I0081417

One Decision Away

Cameron Wheeler

Copyright © 2019

All Rights Reserved

ISBN: 978-1-95-163042-3

Dedication

I would like to thank my mother, Traci Wheeler, for teaching me to guard my heart, and for showing me how to recognize depression and hopelessness in those you love. If it weren't for her raising me the way that she did, I might have never had the idea to write this book, to share my experience, and to inspire others the way I desire to do.

I would also like to thank my grandmother, Dorothy *"Dotty"* Feeley, who taught me compassion. Her zest for life and the love she showed towards her children, her grandchildren, and great-grandchildren taught me invaluable lessons. The emotions that stirred inside were astronomical, to say the least.

These two amazing women left this world far too early. However, before they did, they were able to impart wisdom upon me that I may have never learned from another person, and for this, I am eternally grateful.

What you will find in this book and on the pages that follow, is a collection of my thoughts, my emotions, interactions throughout my day to day life, an entire anthology of my existence on this realm of what we perceive to be the reality. Everything that is written in this volume is meant only to be taken as an inside look into my experience of life. The primary cause what follows on these pages is to hold myself accountable to living the life of continual and upward self-development, which I aspired to lead forward into a more successful and fulfilling life.

This is me, raw and unearthed. Beneath the depth of my mind, my spirit, and my soul, I intend to discover a higher self-awareness, a conscious collective and tap into the universal intelligence. Enjoy the journey.

"If you want something enough, and your heart is pure, wondrous things can happen!"

-Matt Leblanc, playing the role of Joey Tribbiani, T.V.

Show, Friends.

Acknowledgment

The only person I would like to acknowledge is YOU. You are one of those remarkable people who I have authored this book for. There is definitely a spark in you that drove you to opt for this book out of many. Today, you are all set to steer your life towards a positive route. I would like to pay my heartfelt gratitude to you for believing in me and supporting me. I hope my experiences and learnings can bring wisdom and peace in your life as you turn the pages of this book.

About the Author

Cameron currently lives in Mobile, AL and is studying Entrepreneurship at the Mitchell College of Business, University of South Alabama. He has spent the past seven years in the Navy, traveling the world and learning multiple trades along the way. It is his most sincere desire that you will read this book and resonate with his life experiences, be fully interactive with the book, including writing your goals, and apply the teachings within so you can live the life you are designed to live, on your own terms, and without any regrets.

To check out some amazing offers by Cameron Wheeler, you can visit www.camerondwheeler.com. For any queries, ideas, suggestions, and partnerships, you can email him at cameron@camerondwheeler.com. Cameron Wheeler aims to provide a platform where likeminded people can gather and work on the noble cause of changing lives. Connect with him on www.facebook.com/CameronDeeWheeler, and also connect with him on www.instagram.com/camerondeewheeler so that you don't miss out on any updates!

Preface

"The number of ways you can live in one lifetime is limitless. So why limit yourself? The sky is NOT the limit. Beyond the universe is."

-Suzy Kassem

We waste more than half of our lives, focusing on **what we can't do**. We are so busy discouraging ourselves that we don't realize God has blessed us with a special power to change our destinies. This special power resides inside our mind. We have to discover this hidden energy to transform our lives and this world. Finding this potential is the purpose of our lives that we often fail to understand.

Have you ever realized when you focus too much on failure, it keeps chasing you? Do you know why? Because you use your hidden powers incorrectly. You maneuver your entire energy to failure; that's why it takes a hold on you. As Germany Kent says, *"You become what you digest into your spirit. Whatever you think about, focus on, read about, and talk about; you're going to attract more of into your life. Make sure they're all positive."* Life is too short to keep whining about your failures and misfortune. Trials and hardships are an indispensable part of our lives. The real task is to embrace them and never let them destroy you. Life is a competition between you and your tribulations.

Your purpose is to defeat them and keep rising from the ashes.

Contents

Page Left Blank Intentionally

Chapter 1
Early On

People use the terms *"spending your life"* and *"living your life"* interchangeably. In reality, these two terms portray contrasting meanings. When we do not have a vision for our life, we just spend it until our last breath without a purpose. We go where life takes us. This vision is something that tells us the true purpose of our life. When we are sure about our vision, we automatically set goals, and these goals ignite a fire within us. This fire keeps charging us to live our lives to achieve our goals. My life has been no different in this regard. Steve Garvey, a former American baseball player, says:

"You have to set goals that are almost out of reach. If you set a goal that is attainable without much work or thought, you are stuck with something below your true talent and pot."

Now, let me give you an initial perspective of how life began for me *"Early On"*. Life had never been easy for me. Right from my childhood, I had seen those phases of life which many children of such a young age rarely do. These were the times when I could have given up, but the desire to achieve my goals burned deep inside my soul and always lifted me up. Now, when I think about my early life, the trials and tribulations I endured, and the blunders I committed, I feel extremely blissful. Those miseries were blessings in disguise that encouraged me to write this book to motivate you. This book is not only my autobiography; this is the story of everyone who defeated the sufferings of their lives and managed to stay vigorous to achieve their definition of success. It can be you, someone you love, or someone you deeply care about.

When I was about two years old, my parents decided to part ways and got divorced. My father took my brother Kerry along and left me with my mother. Though my brother used to visit us, it wasn't as often as we would like. The first memory that I can remember is from that time. I was crazy for Batman. That Christmas Eve, when my mother gave me a Batman action figure, I was the happiest child in the world and roamed around the entire house playing with it. I had no idea about the cruelties of life that I was going to face in the later years on that day. We used to live in Section 8 housing in Northridge, Virginia Beach. It was an initiative by the US government to provide subsidized housing to financially deprived families. We were the only white family in our neighborhood. Majority of the population there was of the African-American community. Due to this, we were subject to bouts of prejudice from some people in the neighborhood.

I remember one summer when my brother came to visit. Kerry and I were playing in the field next to our house. Some children across the fence were teasing us and calling us names. Then suddenly, they started throwing wooden boards with nails in them across the fence! One of the nails in the board slashed my brothers' arm. Another board hit me in the face, and the nail scratched me in between my eyebrows, nearly missing my eye.

I still have the scar to this day. This was the day when I realized that life was not a bed of roses for us. It was indeed a painful moment for a six-year-old kid. Even today, when I remember the incident, I feel hurt. But I also feel blessed that I experienced the cruelty of life at such a delicate age that turned me into a strong man today. I believe that every moment of our life is planned by our Lord. Whatever miseries we go through make us robust. When I was in the first grade at the age of six, I was diagnosed with Attention-Deficit/Hyperactivity Disorder

(ADHD) and Obsessive-Compulsive Disorder (OCD). ADHD is a psychological disorder that affects young children or teenagers, and it has the tendency to continue even into adulthood. The main symptoms of ADHD are troubles with paying attention, hyperactivity, and the inability to control your impulses. OCD is also a psychological disorder. It includes annoying and distressing feelings, images, or desires that interlope with a child or teen's mind and create anxiety or uneasiness. The patient then attempts to condense by occupying in monotonous actions or behaviors. My mother put me on medications, including pills for treating ADHD.

Those disorders made me lose who I was. It limited my character development. I lost interest in all the activities I once enjoyed. It made me feel like a zombie, walking around with no sense of self or purpose. I remember little from that age as I had become so introverted because of those disorders. The only memory from my first grade is an assignment which I found very interesting. We studied in class to figure out how things get damaged when they fall from a height. Our teacher asked us to take a box, put some eggs in it and drop it from the roof of the gymnasium. When I got home, I took out a box, filled it with as much cotton as I could fit, painted it brown, green, and yellow, and put some eggs in it. The next day I went to class, we all went to the roof, threw our boxes down from there and then came down to check if any eggs were broken. Surprisingly, all the eggs were intensely damaged. A damage which no one could ever repair! This assignment taught me a life lesson; never allow anyone to ruin your heart in a way that it can never again be repaired.

Being a young adult, we often get involved with people who don't care for us much. We give them the authority to treat us in any way they want. My mom taught me to guard my heart to a great degree. She always taught me to be aware of people who only want to use you for their own benefit. We get this life only once, and our own existence is our utmost responsibility. We must learn to love and respect ourselves.

We must never allow people to disrespect us. I don't know whether those psychological disorders made me so sensitive or if something else was the reason behind it. But I would always observe everything that happened in my life thoughtfully. At the age of seven or eight, a child has bountiful desires. Their sparkling eyes are filled with the dreams of getting all their favorite things. But in my case, the greatest happiness was getting timely food. We used to get food from the church or my school. I would walk down Virginia Beach Boulevard, go to the church, and bring home some food for my mother and me. My mother was a patient of chronic depression. When she was 18 years old, she had a motorcycle accident with an 18-wheeler which made her lose her left leg. She could never get over this trauma and confined herself to the bed. At times, she would try to get up and cook food for us. But much of the time, I was the one who was responsible for bringing home the bacon. Though the food I used to bring from the church was never enough for us.

It was a cold day when I was about to go to the church, as usual, to bring the food. To my surprise, a generous man appeared at our doorstep and gave me a jacket. That day I felt rich because it was cold, but I was wearing a warm jacket. Many people complain about not having happiness and prosperity in their life because they don't have a big car or a lavish house. But when I recall these memories, I realize that happiness has a connection with our heart and not with the things we own. The more we get, the more we become ungrateful, as we take things for granted when we own them. Young kids are way more sensitive than adults.

They feel everything in a much more intense manner.

The deprivations of my life keep looping around my mind constantly like a movie. It's been many years, but everything feels like it happened yesterday. Once, when I was around ten years old, my mother and I were sitting at the sidewalk outside our house. We were enjoying a bowl of mixed fruits and watching the sunset. That was a beautiful evening! I enjoyed it immensely because having fresh fruits was a rare occasion for us. My neighbor, Morgan, also came from her house and joined us.

The people in my neighborhood had started to accept me, and I had made many friends. It was one of the most beautiful memories that I can remember from my early days. A pleasant evening, chatting with my mother and friends while relishing the juicy fruits. What else would I want? Suddenly, a car came turning around the corner of the street. It was actually trying to escape another car which was shooting at it. My mother quickly got up and made her way into the house. A guy jumped out of the car, took out his gun, and started shooting down the street. Morgan and I were frightened and filled with fear while seeing the bullets pierce the veil of peace. We quickly ran inside the house and locked ourselves in. It was such a dreadful moment. A peaceful and serene evening turned into a nightmare for us. Though we remained safe at that moment, it took us many days to come back to normal. I felt that my mother was becoming dependent on me over time, and eventually, it was fostering an unhealthy relationship. I was responsible for everything at my home, although I was just eleven years old. However, all those hardships matured me at an early age.

That was the age when I started working after school to bring some money and food at home. Since I was so young, and I didn't know anything else to do, I washed cars, did laundry, and cleaned houses for money. I would work throughout the day, and in the evening, I would bring home bread, milk and eggs. I know many readers can relate to it who have worked hard from an early age. Seeing my friends riding their bikes with no worries while I was working hard to bring in some money was difficult.

Many times, I lost my heart. However, a feeling inside me that *things will get better* uplifted me every time and imbued me with the strength to carry on. When I was in sixth grade, I used to wear a lumberjack style shirt. My classmates would joke about me and made fun of me. They would tease me, but I didn't care. I loved that shirt as it was comfortable and warm. Once I wore that shirt two days in a row, and my classmates made it a big deal calling me names and antagonizing me, *"Poor boy, you wore the same shirt two days in a row!"* They were trying hard to make me lose my temper, but I didn't care at all. After that though, I didn't wear it for two days in a row. When I look back to that, I think no one has the right to change your feelings about yourself. It was such a tender age.

When I was working on my verbal skills, I was also learning who I was. That was the time that taught me that you couldn't trust everyone in life. I learned a great deal from that phase. We oversee our emotions. Happiness is an inside job, one which we must pursue with perseverance and determination.

When I was in seventh grade, I became a member of the Orchestra Club. I was around twelve or thirteen years old at that time. This is the age when teens start to take care of themselves because they can see themselves from another's perspective. One of my classmates suggested that I shave my facial hair. Though at that time, I didn't have much hair on my face, I had started growing a beard and mustache. I figured I'd go along with her idea. When I came back home, I shaved my face. But the funny part is I shaved my face, completely. I even shaved my eyebrows. I know this sounds ridiculous, but I did it anyway out of excitement. Next day I went to school with no eyebrows. Everyone was pointing toward me and laughing. But the girl who suggested to me to shave my face came near to me and said, *"That's sexy"*. I thought she must have been kidding, but she again said, *"That's really sexy"*. She was actually serious about that. What else did I want? I accepted that compliment whole-heartedly. This event taught me another lesson of my life that when you start owning your mistakes and stop taking people's negative comments to heart, you become a better version of yourself. This life is full of tests and trials. So we should try to let go of things that will not affect us in any way.

When I was in ninth grade, I was one of the most popular students in the school. I was around fourteen or fifteen years old. I made plenty of friends, and it was a good time in my life. That is when my school years were about to end, and I was moving toward the next phase of my life. Though this was the end of my school life, it was not the same for my struggles and trials. It was actually a new beginning. I encountered many unexpected circumstances, committed numerous mistakes, and made many flawed decisions with every passing year. But everything taught me a valuable lesson. Each mistake brought me closer to my goals. In the next chapter, I will describe the other nuisances of my life and how I approached those trials to achieve my goals.

Chapter 2
Braving the Storm

The water bubbles gently

Up from the spring of life

New life is given

As the gentle waters flow

Children play and laugh

In the shallow waters

Carefree and joyful

Around a bend the water drifts

Into adolescence

The way grows narrower

The waters swifter

Another small creek

Joins into life's river

Violent rapids form ahead

A fallen tree blocks the way

Debris collects around it

Old bottles and some trash

Polluting the waters.

Little by little

They shake loose

And continue downstream
The problems of adolescence
Left behind.

-Tiffany Chronister

Every phase of life has its own charm and attractions. Childhood is usually the most carefree period of your life when you don't even know the meaning of the word 'Responsibility.' Your parents take care of everything. But I was introduced to this word when I was only six years old. Those were the days when my other friends were worried about their toys and games, but I would struggle to make sure that we had something to eat for dinner.

If I thought life would get easier when I grew up, I was wrong. High school graduation is indeed one of the most beautiful parts of a teen's life. This is the age when the world seems intensely colorful and happening. You want to touch the sky and grab the stars. You plan your career and look forward to your prosperous future. When I graduated high school, things turned quite different for me. When all my friends were excited about their upcoming college life, I was busy thinking about the ways to bring food home. My responsibilities never let me focus on anything else in my life. I had never set any goals. I had no vision of what I wanted to become in my future. I was the youngest in my family in terms of age, but I was the eldest when it came to fulfilling the household responsibilities. Right after graduation, instead of planning about further studies, I decided to find a job because I thought I could improve my lifestyle by earning good money. I had no idea that my cruel life had planned some of the toughest challenges for me.

I began working for Food Lion, that was a grocery store right down the street from my house. I worked there for about a month, and then I quit because I could not perform the menial tasks well on that job. I got my second job at Hardee's. It was a fast-food chain right down the street from my house. I worked there for a year. It was an amazing experience to be a part of Hardees. I learned a great deal at this job. Though Hardees was the best place for working, I realized that I didn't want to work for anybody. I wanted to be an entrepreneur, but I did not have enough finances.

Moreover, I thought I was too young to start my own business. I needed to learn a lot about the ways to make money on my own. I decided to move to Indiana and live with my father. Living in Indiana, I worked at a Dollar General Store for four months and then switched to a car wash facility. While working at the car wash, I met a guy named Red. We became really good friends within a short span of time. Red was a helpful guy who always supported me. He also had a struggling life as I had. Red and I would always try to find new ways to make money. We would sell random stuff and use some portion of our earnings to donate to Goodwill. Those were the days when our financial condition was quite unstable. My brother had been in the Navy as a Hospital Corpsman for the past three years. I also developed an interest to be a part of the Navy. I joined the Navy when I was about twenty years old.

Being in the Navy was entirely different from everything I had ever done in my life before. It was one of the most profound and difficult learning experiences of my life. Navy life during Boot Camp is all about being controlled. You have limited personal choices when you are under training. You have to abide by the rules and say *"Yes"* to every order you get from your Petty Officer or Chief Petty Officer in charge. It was quite difficult for me to adapt to the Navy environment because I had never liked to be answerable to anyone in my life. My responsibilities from such an early age had made me an independent person. I was habitual of doing things in my own way. This attitude made it quite challenging for me to make rank advancements in the Navy. I had adjusted to a whole new structure and discipline. Two months had passed being in the Navy while I was in boot camp. Boot camp is a military training program for new recruits with ruthless discipline. It was extremely grueling and tough. We had to do ten counts, running, push-ups and sit-ups, and other tedious activities. We would sweat profusely. Once a friend of mine at boot camp who was right behind me sweated so much that I slipped in the pool of his sweat.

This was such an unexpected situation that I couldn't keep my balance and accidentally pushed my friend. As a result, his pinky finger fractured. He had to be ASMO'd. ASMO is an acronym for Assignment Memorandum Order. When a recruit is ASMO'd, they are put into a Special Program Division to help them with their fitness or recovery. These programs include Fitness Improvement Training (FIT), Recruit Convalescent Unit (RCU), Fundamental Applied Skills Training (FAST), and Personal Applied Skills Streaming (PASS)[1]. It was a terrible situation for him. He was put back because of that incident. God has created us in such a way that no matter how resistant we are towards change, there comes a time when we accept it. I too became used to Boot camp after a few weeks. It had instilled a lot of discipline within me. I had lost fifteen pounds during my boot camp training. My self-confidence had boosted. Finally, the day came when I graduated from boot camp. It was the month of August 2011.

My father, mother and my mother's boyfriend came to attend my graduation. We all had an amazing day together. After having breakfast, my father and I went back to the hotel and sat in the hot tub for a while. My father was really happy that I had achieved my first milestone in the Navy. It was one of the best days of my life. Though graduating from boot camp was not an out of this world thing, to me, it was like a rainbow after the rainfall. The next stage in the Navy career was CTT schooling. CTT stands for Cryptologic Technician Technical. Under this training, sailors are trained to evaluate classified information and

---

[1]Boot Camp for Navy Families. (2014). ASMO'd – What the heck is ASMO'd?. Website. Retrieved from:https://bootcamp4navyfamilies.wordpress.com/2014/11/19/asmod-what-the-heck-is-asmod/

intelligence[2]. I shipped to Pensacola Florida for the training and stayed there for six months. After that, I moved to Jacksonville, Florida. While in Jacksonville, Florida, I boarded on my first ship, Samuel B. Roberts (FFG-58), as a part of my Navy training. Running dry dock was an enlightening experience. It had been about three months the ship was docked for repairs. We would go to work early in the morning and leave early in the afternoon.

It was a fine Navy day when Mmy phone rang when I was at work. I took my phone out from my pant pocket. My mother was calling me. It had been about five days since I had talked to her. I was glad to see her name on the phone screen. I picked up my phone with a smile, but I was astounded to hear a male voice from the other end. It was not my mother but her boyfriend Mark calling me. He had never called me like this, especially from my mother's phone. My mind alarmed me that something was wrong. My heart was palpitating because of Mark's silence. When he spoke, his words actually shattered my world. He said, *"Cameron, I need you to be strong. I need you to be a*

---

[2]Guerra rapidly. T. (2019). What Can a Navy CTT Do in the Civilian World?. Chron. Retrieved from: https://work.chron.com/can-navy-ctt-civilian-world-21082.html

soldier. Your mother has committed suicide."

It felt like someone had squashed my heart. I couldn't believe that my mother was no more in this world. It was immensely traumatic for me because I had spent a huge part of my life with my mother. She was the one who raised me. My whole world had fallen apart. I was trembling out of grief. Tears rolled down my eyes. Everything in my surroundings seemed to fade away. Mark's words were echoing in my mind. I don't remember how I gathered the courage to go to my petty officer and chief to inform them about the sudden death of my mother. They allowed me to go on emergency leave.

I left from there, and before going to my home, I had visited Wal-Mart and picked up a pack of 24 beers. I drank throughout the night to overcome my grief. The pain of losing my beloved mother was unbearable for me. The next morning when I woke up, I was still drunk. I sobered up enough and got in my car and drove to North Carolina to see my brother Kerry, who lived there with his wife and children. That drive to North Carolina seemed to be the longest drive of my life. Minutes felt like hours. Throughout the drive, I cried crazily. I felt extremely helpless that I didn't have a shoulder to cry on. I wanted to have wings to fly to my brother. When I reached my brother's house, my father had already arrived there from Indiana to console us during this devastating time. We didn't have enough energy to plan her funeral until a couple of days before. We were so traumatized that we really needed time to calm our nerves down. We tried to compose ourselves by reminiscing her good memories and playing board games for some time.

Eventually, we were at the point where we had to gather money for her funeral. It was heartbreaking to think about my mother turning into ashes. But we had to do it. We held her funeral at the church I used to get food from when I was young. It was a beautiful funeral. There were plenty of my friends at the church who had come to attend the last rituals of my mother. My heart tore into pieces when I saw my mother's ashes on the altar.

I awake each morning to start a new day,
But the pain of losing you never goes away.
I go about the things I have to do,
And as the hours pass, I think again of you.
I want to call you and just hear your voice.
Then I remember that I have no choice
For you are not there and now my heart cries

Just to see you again to tell you goodbye.
To say, Mama, I love you and I always will
And hope that much of you, in me you've instilled.
The day that you left, I just didn't know
That you were going where I couldn't go.
And now all my memories of you are so dear
But gosh, how I miss you and wish you were here.
Who now can hear me when I need to cry?
It's so hard to tell you, "Mama Goodbye."
Someday I know all will be well
And I'll see you again with stories to tell
Of how you were missed and how we have grown
And how good it is to finally be home.
Until then my memories of you I'll keep near
And I'll pass them on to those who are dear.

-Claudia Lee

No matter how big your loss is, you have to move on. This is the rule of this cruel life because you have no other option. Your friends and companions console you for the initial few days, then everybody forgets about your suffering. Only you are the one who endures this pain throughout your life. After my mother's funeral, we all tried to get back to our normal lives. I pretended to be normal, but I was not. It was awfully difficult for me to accept this reality. I would drink alcohol every night in a hope to ease my pain. One day when I went to work, I was drunk. I couldn't concentrate on my work. My leading Petty Officer came to me and said,

"Hey, you got to go home. Go and sleep it off and make sure this never happens again."

I went home that day and slept it all off. I realized that day what I had been doing was not okay. It was damaging my life. I had decided to overcome this damaging habit, but nothing changed much. I would still drink every night. I was in search of love and affection. This was the reason that I got into the destructive habit of filling up my time with temporary women who I never wanted to be with.

I would spend my time with them to have sexual pleasure. It was fun to be with different women and drinking all the time. Now when I look back, I realize I could have set productive goals instead of wasting my time with those women. I wasted the first three years of my Navy career drinking and hanging out with friends purposelessly. I was completely ignorant of my health. I had gained a lot of weight. I was about two hundred and twenty pounds at that time. My life ran on the same path.

Suddenly, there came a turning point in my life. I was twenty-four years old when I was exposed to a highly renowned marketing company.

My dream of becoming an entrepreneur could turn into reality. I decided to quit drinking with firm determination. I dabbled with that company with a business perspective. My role was to expand the network of people for that company. I was extremely positive and dedicated. After my mother's death, it was the first time I had taken an interest in anything. Things were falling in place.

I was hopeful for a better future. When I got into the company, I had completely quit drinking and wasting my time with temporary people. But after a few months, I had reverted to my destructive habits. I failed my business targets miserably. I would drink alcohol throughout the day and spend every night with those temporary women. I never thought about getting into a serious relationship because I was not mentally prepared.

I was well aware that those temporary women had no affection for me, yet I was wasting my time for them. I was walking around life with no purpose. Alcohol had become medicine for me. I would take it to release my pain temporarily. I knew alcohol had damaged my physical and mental health, but I was helpless. It was nearly impossible for me to live without alcohol and women. Every day when I woke up in the morning, I would wonder where my life was taking me to. I was clueless. I didn't have any motivation left in my life. In 2015, I cross-rated to Aviation Structural Mechanic - Safety Equipment also called AME. I was twenty-five years old at that time. I would still use alcohol, but not so much to drown away the pain. It had become an addiction for me now. Whenever I had a feeling of boredom sitting in my room after work, I would drink alcohol and play a video game.

Eventually, my interest in alcohol, women, and video games began fading away. I had had enough of that. I would not feel pleasure in those activities anymore. I started looking for ways to improve my life. For the first time in my life ever, I had developed an interest in meditation and therapy. At that point, my life turned its way towards a positive change.

Chapter 3
Your Most Valuable Resource

If only I could rewind and go back in my mind

Seek it out then destroy would I truly enjoy

Would my life now be good like I feel that it should

Or would things just get worse am I blessed am I cursed

Will things settle and go will my happiness grow

Or will things get real bad making me very sad

To rewind in my mind might well make me unkind

Maybe leave it alone and rejoice, not condone

Sometimes you're better off where you are

Don't look back you may go far

Life's a gamble choose your way well

What will happen time will tell

If I rewind my heart would it feel torn apart

Would the heartache it holds disappear or twofold

Would I feel some release maybe panic would cease

Or would things just get worse am I blessed am I cursed

Will I find myself love and then reach on above?

Or will my heart still ache through the choices I make

To rewind my heart might well tear me apart

Maybe leave it alone and rejoice, not condone
Sometimes you're better off where you are
Don't look back you may go far
Life's a gamble choose your way well
What will happen time will tell
If I rewind my life would it free me from strife
Would my fears melt away leave me happy today
Would my happiness flow if my memories go
Or would things just get worse am I blessed am I cursed
Will I ever be free to truly know me
Or will life carry on without rhyme or reason
To rewind my life would I not be a wife
Maybe leave it alone and rejoice, not condone

-Jane Shields

How would it feel, if you had an eraser to rub out the bad chapters from the book of your life?

Everything would be perfect then!

You could correct everything you have ever done incorrectly. You could fix the bad decisions you have made. You could make up for the time you have wasted. But unfortunately, no such option is available to us. Whatever has happened can never be altered. I have wasted a lot of time in my life because of my destructive habits. Deep down in my heart, I had the regret of not being with my mother when she had been all alone. I badly wanted to travel back in time to see my mother, but some wishes can never be granted. I had been living a purposeless life. The only things which would give me temporary pleasure were alcohol and women. Eventually, such pleasures faded out. At this time, I realized that I needed to do something to change my life. I found a way to work through it with meditation and therapy. It was not an overnight job. It took me a great deal of effort and time. Instead of trying to suppress my pain using alcohol and women, I researched about the ways to use meditation as a tool for finding inner peace.

It was a long and tedious journey, but it completely transformed my life. When I was going through my therapy sessions, I realized how much pain my mother must have endured. She had already attempted suicide twice now. I had been quite young when she had made such attempts. Still, I left her alone and got into my own world. My miseries have taught me a lesson that your family is your strongest support system. You must never underestimate it. In my marathon to improve my lifestyle, I had been disconnected from my family for too long, especially from my mother, who had always been dependent on me. My life had coached me that suicide attempts were a sign that your loved ones needed your attention and presence. We take our closest relationships for granted. We only realize their true value when we lose them. When I was on my journey to change my life, I noticed that the biggest problem in our life is we can't manage our time well. Our priorities change in every phase of our lives. For example, when we are kids, we are too attached with our parents, and we love to spend most of our time with them, but when we grow up, we get more into friends and outings. As a result, our parents feel ignored and neglected. There is nothing wrong in exploring the world as a part of growing up. The problem arises when we fail to create a balance among different priorities of our lives.

Time is indeed the most valuable resource we have been blessed with. I am growing my business now with total focus on my vision and goals. When I look back, I feel remorse about wasting my time on alcohol and women. I could have laid the foundation of my business years ago if I had not gotten into those damaging habits. I would have much more experience under my belt, had I not made the excuse of using alcohol instead of facing my problems. I had to pay a huge price to realize the importance of time, but I want my readers to learn from my experiences. I will share how I settled my business in the later chapters of this book. I want my readers to know how managing time efficiently helped me in achieving my goals. When I had been addicted to alcohol, I could not concentrate on anything in my life. We believe that addiction is confined to alcohol and drugs only, but the reality is quite different. There are several other things in our lives which don't seem to be an addiction, but they really are. One of the most enslaving things these days in our lives is social media. Yes, you read it right. Social media has taken a strong hold on our lives. We usually wake up to our phone alarms and then dive into the world of endless notifications from Facebook, Instagram, Snapchat, WhatsApp, Twitter, and other similar applications.

Our life has become so virtual that when we go out for a picnic or for dinner with family and friends, our sole attraction is to click some tantalizing pictures and to upload them on social media platforms to get maximum likes. We are no more interested in family talks and gossip. Even while hanging out with one another, every member of the family is busy looking down at their phones. A few days back, my Facebook app crashed. I was amazed to notice that within an hour's time, I had gone back and tried to open up the application about eleven times. It happens with the majority of us. We check our Facebook and Instagram apps over a hundred times in a day, even when we don't have any notifications. I believe this is one of the biggest time-wasters. Many of my friends spend several hours surfing their phones and liking their friends' posts on Instagram and Facebook. They feel great pleasure in retweeting things that don't really serve any purpose to them. When we use social media in the wrong ways, we constantly expose ourselves to lifestyles of the people who are in our friend list.

We begin comparing our lives to our friend's lives subconsciously. This behavior leads us to a feeling that we are not worth as much as someone else is. I don't mean to communicate that we must not use social media. It has truly become an indispensable part of our lives. People run their businesses through social media pages and groups. We can grow our professional network from these platforms. However, we must limit the time to use these applications. Moreover, these applications in themselves are not good or bad, but the way we use them turns them into productive or destructive. One of the best things that helped me a lot in overcoming my social media addiction was logging out of these applications from time to time.

We keep ourselves logged in constantly to make sure that we don't miss out on any important messages or updates from any of our friends. The reality is that if someone really wants to contact us, they can call us or text us at any time. There is no need for us to stay logged in to our social media accounts 24/7. When you disconnect yourself from the virtual world, it helps you in reconnecting to the other areas of your life.

We feel proud that we have thousands of followers and friends on our social media accounts, but are they actually our friends? We don't talk to most of the people who are added to our friend list. Ever since I have begun steering my life towards a positive change, I use social media for my business purposes mostly.

I believe that meeting new people in person and growing your real network is more effective than adding people you barely know on Facebook or Instagram. It is said that we are the combination of the five people we spend most of our time with. I believe this to be a hundred percent true.

The people in your surroundings have a huge impact on your life. They play a vital role in shaping your personality. The best way to grow your network is to attend seminars and conferences. It will benefit you in two ways. Firstly, it will prove to be an enlightening experience for you which will enhance your knowledge. Secondly, you will get an opportunity to meet and be friends with different influential people. I got a chance to speak with a very intelligent and powerful woman in late October of 2019. She agreed to mentor me over the next couple of months for some time. I take it as an achievement because not everyone gets the privilege of learning from the experiences of renowned people. I switched my interest from social networking sites to real networking events, and it made a real difference for me. Being social and extrovert is a great way to reach out to the people of power and influence.

These are the people who can inspire and help you in achieving your goals. When you get to know about the struggles and hardships these people faced to reach every milestone in their lives, you feel determined to work towards achieving the ultimate goal of your life. People usually complain about not having enough time. Have you ever thought about people who go from rags to riches?

How did they accomplish their goals? Did they have more than twenty-four hours a day? God has bestowed every human being with only twenty-four hours, yet some are more successful than others who are busy complaining about their struggles. Successful people know how to manage their time well. They maintain their personal and professional relationships efficiently because they are experts in time management.

Grant Cardone is one of the most popular speakers, a best-selling author, and a real estate mogul. During his speaking sessions, he emphasizes a lot on time management. He believes that we can't manage time until we create it ourselves. In one of his articles he said,

"Create time; don't manage it. Divide each hour into four 15-minute blocks of time and see how much you can complete in each 15-minute block. Work fast and furiously to see how much you can accomplish—make it a game. When you start to approach time this way, you start to move from one thing to the next with little room for disruption[3]."

---

[3]Cardone. G. (2017). How to Make this Holiday Season Your Best Ever. LinkedIn. Retrieved from: https://www.linkedin.com/pulse/how-make-holiday-season-your-best-ever-grant-cardone/

I found this idea very catchy and workable. I try to implement this rule in my life. I put things into fifteen-minute blocks. This way, I can explore several new horizons. For example, I can make ten phone calls in fifteen minutes and expose my products and services to ten new people. Other than properly using social media, the most important thing that has helped me a lot is maintaining my to-do-list. I have a planner in which I write everything down. I schedule my meetings weeks and sometimes even months in advance because that way, I ensure that this schedule is non-negotiable. If someone tries to schedule something else with me at the last minute, I can straightaway apologize without any ambiguity. I have about 35 to 40 different alarms set in my phone, so I can have a reminder to do specific things such as getting up early in the morning, to meditate, and to read for at least an hour a day. I have also installed the Amazon Alexa app on my phone. I use this app to remind me about things such as writing an important paper or making a phone call to one of my peers.

You may have noticed that everything I have suggested to you revolved around my phone. See, in this scenario, I am using this new technology for productive uses instead of using it for wasting my time. Instead of checking my notifications or playing some useless games, I am using technology to line things up for me. Whenever we talk about gearing life towards positivity, the first thing we talk about is goal-setting. It is indeed the most important factor, but we can set goals only when we have time to think about them. That is the reason I believe in time management or time creation which comes first of all in all our priorities.

"Time = life; therefore, waste your time and waste of your life, or master your time and master your life."

-Alan Lakein

Chapter 4
Lessons from Abroad

"All travel has its advantages. If the passenger visits better countries, he may learn to improve his own. And if fortune carries him to worse, he may learn to enjoy it."

-Samuel Johnson

How do you prioritize traveling in your life?

For many of us, traveling often seems like a luxury to indulge in once in a while if we can. In fact, a vast majority of people don't travel at all in their youth because they believe that one should travel only after retirement. It is something many of us enjoy and think about, but don't always get around to. Moreover, we hardly consider the benefits it possesses in terms of our health.

Traveling does have the potential to make us healthier, both physically and psychologically. We may not be actively aware of it, but traveling can bring about substantive positive changes, which can take effect both during the course of travel and over the longer term. Being a child who belonged to a financially deprived family, I had never even dreamed about traveling. But our life is more like a roller coaster; it always takes unexpected turns. As a part of the Navy, I had been fortunate enough to have a chance to visit different countries and explore unique cultures and places. But I want to communicate to my readers that if you really want to learn something when you travel, you must avoid alcohol as much as you can. Alcohol slows down your mental activity. It turns you so lethargic that you can't focus on anything around you. In this chapter, I will share my traveling experience and the learnings associated with my journey.

Italy:

"Italy is a dream that keeps returning for the rest of your life."

-Anna Akhmatova

I have been to Italy seventeen times during the course of my life. However, there was a huge difference between my first and seventeenth visit. When I had visited Italy for the first time, I used to have an addictive personality. I would begin with one glass of wine and then couldn't stop drinking until I had lost my mind completely. My friends and I would walk around different places to get some drinks.

We had no interest in exploring the culture and communicating with people. However, over the next several visits, my focus and interest had been shifted from drinking to going out and seeing the culture. When I visited Italy for the fourteenth time, my friends and I went to see the sprawling beauty of Rome. We got a glimpse of beautiful fountains. While walking along the street, we stopped at a restaurant that had twenty-five different species of fishes available. They cooked the fresh fish right in front of us and served us. It was a quite unique experience for me because I had never seen anything like this before. Another thing which inspired me a lot was the liveliness of this royal place. People would gather around the fountains to exhibit their performances. They would perform magic tricks or would dance and sing poetries. I loved watching them do what they were passionate about.

It usually happens that when people travel abroad, they avoid talking to new people because they think they are strangers. Most of the times people stick to themselves and hence cannot get the most out of their expedition. I have learned during my last few trips that communicating with different people actually opens up your mind. You make new friends. You get to know about their experiences. It actually broadens your perspective about the world. It directs you about your goals. Italy's architecture and huge buildings captured my attention. We had a guided tour to the ancient Roman city Pompeii where we walked around the streets. There was a spot on the ground where I saw a phallic-shaped object. It was really surprising for me. I went close, and it was actually a penis carved into the stone on the ground which pointed in the direction of the brothel. These carvings had been created for the men who would be drunk and stumbled on the ground.

When they saw the penis-shaped object on the ground, they would know which direction they must move to be with women at the brothel. The guide took us to the ground where we followed the direction pointed by the penis carvings. It was hilarious. We checked into the brothel where we encountered another amusing thing. The brothel had little carvings of different positions that women would do in different rooms. People could decide which room to go to get a specific type of pleasure. I never knew that something like this could have existed. It was a funny yet creative experience. The most magnetizing thing throughout the Pompei was the remains of the volcanic eruptions of Mt. Vesuvius.

When Mt. Vesuvius had overflown, it had petrified the people living nearby people in stone and ash. We saw a man's body who had been petrified into ash and stone, and it was in a glass casing. Seeing these ashes made me realize that life is really unpredictable. Within a moment, the cruel volcano turned the people into ashes. It made me value my life a lot more at that time.

We also visited a church named Saint Peter's in Italy. The artwork on its ceilings was truly spellbinding. I couldn't take my eyes off this creative art for a several hours. The creative genius of men to come together and create such beautiful works of art instilled such intense levels inspiration within me.

Spain:

"In Spain, the dead are more alive than the dead of any other country in the world."

-Federico Garcia Lorca

Spain is undoubtedly one of the best countries in the world. The great food, people, art, culture, and architecture of Spain are the biggest attraction for the tourists. Once during my time in the Navy, our ship pulled into Rota, Spain. I gathered up my friends, and we got off the ship. We wanted to get something to eat, so we went out. That was the time when I had been struggling to quit drinking. While walking around the streets of Spain, we got to see a lot of beautiful things, especially the clothing which people had been selling, which were quite unique and fascinating. I had never seen such clothes in America.

We stopped at a restaurant to have dinner. The restaurant resembled a wooden canopy, and it was overlooking the coast. I ordered the main course which looked like chicken soup, but it was the most delicious thing I have ever had. After dinner, we decided to have Sangria. The specialty of that restaurant was that they let us create our own Sangria with different types of juices. It was an awesome experience sitting on the beach and creating our own drinks. My friends and I still relish this delightful memory whenever we catch up.

After being done with dinner and drinks, we decided to go to a strip club. We ended up getting in a taxi, thanks to a man outside of a bar. We all were drunk at that time but still in our senses. The taxi driver had told us that it would take us ten minutes to reach our destination, but he had been roaming for thirty minutes, and still, we could see no signs of our destination. His expressions seemed quite shady. Suddenly, in the rearview I saw a vison of the man who hailed us the taxi, and he was following us very closely. We felt that he had been trying to abduct us. One of my friends grabbed the driver from the back seat and asked him strictly to turn the car immediately. The driver flipped a U-turn quickly and then dropped us to the point from where we had got in the taxi. It was a terrible experience for us in a new country. We got back to the ship safely. If we had been overly drunk that day, we could have never stopped the taxi driver from abducting us. I still thank God for getting us back to the ship safe and sound.

Greece:

    "Greece is the most magical place on Earth."

-Kylie Bax

Greece is famous for the thousands of islands dotting the three seas that surround the country. One of the most beautiful things that I remember about Greece was sunset and sunrise. It looked over the water as if a new sun had been brought to the world. It was something I had never seen before in my life. I also enjoyed a 19-mile bike ride throughout Greece which took me a couple of hours with several of my shipmates and some locals. We were in Souda Bay and went from the bottom of the mountain all the way to the top. We got to see little houses, restaurants, and bars and it was a quite enjoyable experience. We had been riding uphill for probably seven miles, and once we reached the top of the mountain, we could view the entire beach. It was an eye-catching sight. We went further up and got to the peak of the mountain. The view from the peak was captivating. It seemed like the aerial view of all of Greece. I captured some amazing pictures of the view. I had never imagined in my childhood that I could have ever got the opportunity to explore these tantalizing places.

I visited a place named Dr. Fish to get a fish pedicure. I had experienced it for the first time in my life, and it was fun. I can still feel the tickling in my feet. I went to a barbershop to get a haircut. The shop was located upstairs in a building. I checked in and sat on a chair. A lady showed up with a glass of beer in her hands. She presented that glass to me. It was their custom to welcome their customers like that. I loved this respectful gesture. While I had been enjoying the beer, the lady gave me a relaxing shoulder massage and put a hot towel around my neck. We had traveled throughout the day, and this massage eased up my muscles. The lady then gave me a nice haircut. I loved the way she would treat her customers. We had been staying at a hotel that was right across the street from the beach. The coolest thing about the hotel was its outside tower.

The tower had different levels where you could go and get an exotic massage. There was also a small bar right downstairs adjacent to the entrance of the hotel. The most fascinating thing about this bar was that there was a small pool where we could swim under the bar and see the bartender make the drinks for us. Though these things must be quite unusual for the people who frequently travel, for me, every experience was unique and memorable.

Scotland:

"Scotland is the Canada of England!"

-Rainn Wilson

A couple of my friends and I had been out to the sea for

about 43 days. Our ship had been heading towards Scotland because we needed a part for the ship. We pulled into Scotland, but the part we needed was not vacant at the time. We had to stay for about two weeks in Scotland. The dollar to pound exchange rate was 1.52, so we had been spending 50 percent more than what we had originally planned. After roaming there for about a week, everybody was back on the ship because they had spent all their money on alcohol and food.

I had worked in the foreign exchange trading industry for some time, so I already had an idea about the fluctuating exchange rates of Scotland. Right from the first day, I had decided that I would not drink every night. So instead of wasting my money on alcohol, I spend most of my time exploring the beauty of this country. I went to Edinburgh and Rural Scotland. We would get on the train and then travel out. We saw a castle which was an epitome of magnificence. We didn't actually go inside.

We just had a view of the ridges of the castle. I still remember that mesmerizing sight. It felt like a scene from a movie. I saw a deer poking its head out of the bushes. I also caught sight of squirrels running around. The trees had been so shiny and bright, and it seemed like glitter had been falling from them. From there we went into the town to have our dinner. I still feel the taste of the Macaroni and cheese in my mouth that I had enjoyed in Scotland. It was the most amazing Mac and cheese I had ever had. After dinner, we had been walking around the streets and eventually we had ended up into a bar where we played snooker. While we had been having a couple of drinks, one of the local guys got into an argument with one of our sailors.

The local guy smashed a bottle over our sailor's head. There was complete chaos in the bar. Ultimately we had to get out of there because the locals had called the police and we didn't want to be a part of any conflict. We hightailed it back to the ship where one of our senior leaders told us that this bar was blacklisted. He advised us to avoid going there again. However, a few of my friends still went there and faced similar consequences as we had before.

My every expedition was full of some exciting and some unexpected events. Every tour was full of lessons. I made new friends, I learned how to manage difficult situations, and the most important thing was I learned to overcome my alcohol addiction. During our stay in Scotland, I encountered a consignment shop which had been famous for selling used clothes. I bought a Puma sweatshirt, a knit cap, and some gloves because it had been pretty cold out there. Though it had been a used sweatshirt, I fell in love with Puma from that point. Some of my friends also competed with the Scottish Navy in a gym. They set some new records for deadlifting and bench-press. I had felt so proud of my friends for their glorified victory.

Israel:

"Israel is beautiful – and it's the place where the stories of the Bible actually took place."

-Michael Lichtenstein

Another favorite country where I had been to, along with my peers was Israel. We docked out at Haifa, and our commanding officers asked us not to shave while we were in Haifa. They didn't want us to be easily identifiable. In Israel, we were free from shaving our beards. We could blend in well. We would walk around the streets like common travelers due to operational security purposes.

I came across a beautiful religious tradition at Israel. There was a wall where people would go, write a small wish on a piece of paper, fold the paper, and put it inside the wall. People believed that their prayers would be answered this way. I also got the opportunity to go to Jerusalem and visit the site, which is renowned as the crucifying place of Jesus Christ. It was an immensely spiritual experience. I felt the presence of God there. There had been little tunnels and paths that would lead people to the actual stone where Jesus had been laid. They would allow people to touch that stone. When I put my hand on the stone, it enriched me with a surreal religious and spiritual experience. I felt I had received some unique power. I prayed for the health and wellbeing of the people I had loved. Then I got up and walked away. From that moment I felt a change within myself. I felt I had a purpose in life.

This experience developed an entrepreneurial spirit in me. Before that point, I had tried to get into different types of business ventures, but I had failed because I didn't have any true purpose behind it. But at that moment I felt that I had a higher calling in life. I developed a determination to do something that would add value to the world. This experience really opened my eyes, my heart, and my soul to discover the newer possibilities of achieving something in life. My traveling experiences proved to be a turning point in my life. When I visited Israel, I didn't find alcohol, and when I visited other countries, I tried to avoid alcohol myself so that I could enjoy the culture and beauty of these countries. I believe it was a testament that I had much more to achieve in my life than wasting it on alcohol only.

"The mystery of human existence lies not in just staying alive, but in finding something to live for."

-Fyodor Dostoyevsky

Chapter 5
Become an Opportunist

"We are so accustomed to the comforts of 'I cannot,' 'I do not want to' and 'it is too difficult' that we forget to realize when we stop doing things for ourselves and expect others to dance around us, we are not achieving greatness. We have made ourselves weak."

-Pandora Poikilos

When a powerful woman offered to me to be my mentor, I didn't know I had stumbled upon a great opportunity. I grabbed it immediately. Her guidance and mentorship played a vital role in transforming my life.

What if I had not tried to interact with her?

What if I had not accepted her as my mentor?

I might be living the same purposeless life which I had been spending years ago. I made use of an opportunity that came my way in a timely manner. Becoming an opportunist is the key to bring a positive change in your life. Now the question arises what does it mean to be an opportunist?

According to Oxford Learner's Dictionaries, *"An opportunity is a time when a particular situation makes it possible to do or achieve something[4]"* and *"An opportunist is a person who makes use of an opportunity, especially to get an advantage[5]."*

From the perspective of an opportunist, you will notice that each day of your life brings numerous opportunities to you, which keep multiplying when you avail them. When I got a chance to interact with the woman who spoke with such conviction, I was quite hesitant. However, I stepped out of my comfort zone and talked to her because that was an opportunity which I may never have received later in my life.

Though I had never expected that someone like her, whose time was literally her money, would agree to become a guide and coach to me. My opportunity to speak to her gave me a chance to stay in touch with her. Staying

---

[4]Oxford Learner's Dictionaries. (2019). Definition of opportunity noun from the Oxford Advanced American Dictionary. Website. Retrieved from: https://www.oxfordlearnersdictionaries.com/definition/american_english/opportunity

[5]Oxford Learner's Dictionaries. (2019). Definition of opportunist noun from the Oxford Advanced Learner's Dictionary. Website. Retrieved from: https://www.oxfordlearnersdictionaries.com/definition/english/opportunist_1?q=opportunist

in touch with her allowed me the opportunity to become her mentee. That's how opportunities multiply constantly. People generally resist change. Many times, they lose their best chance only because they didn't want to get out of the bubble they have created for themselves. They miss out on many opportunities because they fear failure or rejection. Therefore, people prefer staying in their comfort zone rather than exploring something new.

Richard Branson is an entrepreneur. He is the founder of the Virgin group of companies. As a child, Richard struggled with dyslexia. He was a below-average student during his school life. He was more interested in extracurricular activities, such as football and cricket. At the age of 16, Richard dropped out of school and moved to London to start his own magazine about youth culture named The Student.

This magazine was run by students, and it attracted significant advertisement from firms wishing to tap into a market of student consumers. He distributed the first 50,000 copies of the magazine for free. He then set up a mail-order company named Virgin to harmonize with The Student magazine. Richard never stopped exploring new opportunities. He kept on growing his business, and today,

Virgin is a diversified group of over 400 private companies. He has a current net worth of USD 4 billion[6]. Richard says,

"If somebody offers you an amazing opportunity, but you are not sure you can do it, say yes – then learn how to do it later!"

To create a fulfilling life, it is necessary that you expand your personal boundaries. Successful people never fear accepting challenges and embracing risks. They not only transform their own lives but also pave the way for others to follow. Here are some of the advantages of moving out of your comfort zone.

Unlimited Growth

When you are committed to embracing challenges, you reach the peak of your performance level. If you stay stuck to your routine lifestyle, you can never expect to evolve and touch the height of success. You may do well till a certain level, but you can never stand out in a crowd. When you break free from the shackles of mediocrity, you find countless ways to grow and improve.

---

[6]Biography Online. (2019). Richard Branson, Biography. Website. Retrieved from: https://www.biographyonline.net/business/richard_branson.html

Self-Awareness

Taking risks will not only open up the doors of success for you, but it will also help you in becoming aware of yourself. It will enlighten you about your aptitudes, interests, and strengths. Trying something new helps you in identifying your hidden prospects. When you achieve something you once thought was impossible, your self-confidence boosts up. You become more assertive about your abilities. It increases your passion for learning and discovering new horizons.

Ability to Deal with Challenges

You can never predict what will happen in the next moment. When you are equipped with a variety of skills and habitual of facing risks, you can easily manage the trials and tribulations of life. People who never strive to break through their limits always complain about their misfortune and adversities.

Adventurous Life

People who keep repeating the same tasks on a daily

basis soon get tired of their constant routine. When you experience new possibilities and broaden your perspectives, your life becomes more interesting and worth living. You don't feel purposeless. It creates a sense of self-satisfaction within yourself.

Relationship Building

When you step out of your comfort zone, you get a chance to know yourself. We spend most of our lives in pleasing and nurturing our relationships with the people in our surroundings. It is indeed a good habit, but the most important person in your life is YOU. If you are not happy with yourself, trying to please your family and friends is nearly useless. Loving yourself is the key to a successful life.

When you extend your boundaries, you become self-aware. You develop a better idea of what makes you happy. This magnifies your self-confidence, which will eventually help you in building a strong relationship with people around you. I want my readers to understand that you are always one decision away from an entirely different life. Therefore, it is mandatory to make that decision carefully. When I joined the navy, I was originally supposed to be a

Master at Arms. I had a $20,000 enlistment bonus which I was supposed to get. However, somehow, my recruiter lost my paperwork, and I ended up moving to Indiana. Now I think, if he hadn't lost my paperwork, I would have been a Master at Arms. I would be in a different country right now with a different rate. Even after my paperwork was lost if I had chosen to stay in Virginia, I would have probably reverted to old destructive habits. My decision to move to Indiana and stay with my father completely altered my life.

I believe it was one of the best decisions of my life. It recalibrated my outlook on life. I joined the Navy and became a Cryptologic Technician. This opportunity led me to grow my network of positive people and develop resilience in my personality. Following are some of the ways which can help you in stepping out of your comfort zone.

Discover What Is out of Your Comfort Zone

What are some of the activities that fascinate you, but you never indulge in them because of the fear of possible failure and disappointment? Take a paper, draw a circle, and write the things which you frequently do or on a daily basis inside the circle. The next step is to write those things which you want to do but have not tried yet because you think you can't do it. This process will help you in identifying your comforts and discomforts. If you like something and think that you are not capable of doing it, it may be your false perception about yourself. When we find any activity attractive, it depicts that we have the potential to do it.

Identify the Reason Behind Your Discomforts

Once you have listed down the things inside and outside of the circle, the next step is to analyze the factors which keep certain things outside your comfort zone. Why are you afraid of trying something which you find interesting? There can be several reasons. You may have a fear of failure. You may have communication apprehension. You may be insecure if being ignored. You may be concerned about your finances. Be honest with yourself while assessing the reason behind your discomfort.

Get Comfortable with Discomfort

When you drew the circle, you listed all your comforts inside the circle and discomforts outside the circle. One of the best ways to get comfortable with your discomforts is to expand your circle. Identify the possible consequences if you fail. Try to read the life stories of successful people who never gave up even after numerous failures. If they can do it, why can't you? Your fears must not become a hindrance in your road to success. We are not born to be conquered by our fears but to defeat our fears.

Consider Failure as a Teacher

Instead of losing hope and giving up, begin considering failure as a teacher. Failures are a great way to be aware of your own strengths and weaknesses. Failure is a great experience, which gives you a lesson to increase the chances of success in your next adventure. Wipe out the fear of failure from your heart because this fear paralyzes your self-esteem. When people are afraid of something, they think that they are not courageous. However, courage is not the absence of fear. Courage is the presence of fear and acting upon what you're afraid of regardless.

Take Small Steps

Don't try to jump outside of your comfort zone overnight. This is what the majority of people do. As a result, they feel overwhelmed and believe that they don't have true potential. It is always better to take baby steps. For example, if you want to become a writer, it is not recommended to begin with writing your own book. I will suggest you get a hang on it by writing small blogs and articles. Once you learn the necessary techniques, you can step ahead further.

Build a Network with Risk-Takers

There is no alternative to this step. If you want to excel at something, it is always beneficial to be in a company of those people who have experienced risks, failures, and rejections. They can help you with their own experiences. If you can't find any risk-takers around you, you can benefit from the internet. You can find thousands of videos and articles about the real-life stories of celebrities and famous personalities. You can also read the books by renowned entrepreneurs and businessmen who embraced failures and emerged as a successful individual. Their influence will begin having a positive impact on your behavior.

Be Honest with Yourself

When you don't feel comfortable in doing something, never say, *"I don't have time"* or *"I will try it later."* Instead, be honest with yourself and admit that you are afraid of doing it. God has designed every human being with flaws. Your weaknesses don't make you a loser. However, avoiding your fears and weaknesses can be an obstacle for your success.

Identify How Stepping out Will Benefit You

How will your writing skills benefit you? Ask this question to yourself and analyze the potential benefits. Keep these interests in mind as motivations to push through fear.

Focus on the Fun

Learn to laugh at yourself when you make mistakes. Risk-taking will inevitably involve failure and setbacks that will sometimes make you look foolish to others. Be happy to roll with the punches when others poke fun. Enjoy the process of stepping outside your safe boundaries. Enjoy the fun of discovering things about yourself that you may not have been aware of previously.

Law of Attraction

I believe in the law of attraction and love. *"The Law of Attraction is the ability to attract into our lives whatever we are focusing on. It is believed that regardless of age, nationality, or religious belief, we are all susceptible to the laws which govern the Universe, including the Law of Attraction. It is the Law of Attraction which uses the power of the mind to translate whatever is in our thoughts and materialize them into reality*[7].*"*

You attract what you are and what you believe in. If you consistently think negatively, you will face negative outcomes. So it's important to redefine their beliefs and basically build up a solid level of ethics and responsibilities

---

[7]The Law of Attraction. (2019). What Is The Law Of Attraction? Open Your Eyes To A World Of Endless Possibilities. Website. Retrieved from: http://www.thelawofattraction.com/what-is-the-law-of-attraction/

and to abide by your morals. Your moral compass needs to be completely in line with what you decide to become. It was May 2015. I used to pay $460 a month for my car loan. It was indeed a huge amount for me. I always thought of the ways to get rid of this car payment. One day, I went to a barbershop. I parked my car, got out of it, and went inside. Two minutes later, a blue van smashed into the back of my car and totaled it. I was shocked to see my car smashing through the barbershop window. I immediately got up and went outside. I found out that the van driver had a heart attack, and this was the reason he lost control. The police told me that if I had not parked my car there, the van would have ran through the entire store and killed about twelve to fourteen people. I didn't care about my car.

I was only worried about the safety of people. This accident wiped away all my debt. I claimed the insurance. Though it took a few months to pay off, eventually all the debts were paid off, and I got another car. I believe it was the law of attraction that combined with the frequency of my thoughts and put it into the universe. You must always believe in your abilities and think positive. Your life is greatly affected by your beliefs and perceptions. No one is going to believe in you more than you believe in yourself.

"Set a goal to achieve something that is so big, so exhilarating that it excites you and scares you at the same time."

-Bob Proctor

I actually learned this from Bob Proctor that you should carry a goal card of your ultimate mission statement and life purpose. Every day you should read this out loud to yourself to reaffirm and understand what your life purpose is. Based on your purpose, you should continuously strive to achieve your goals. If you read this goal card daily and abide by it, you will have no option other than to achieve it.

It can instill the belief in yourself that this is something which can truly change your life. Eventually, you begin applying these things in your life and develop the desired traits and characteristics in yourself. There is no hard and fast rule to set your goals. You can start by writing down the ten most important goals of your life, or you can set your daily goals. Begin your day by writing down your goal of the day and then focus on achieving it. At the end of the day, assess your performance. Initially, you may find it a little challenging, but with daily practice, you can be an expert. It is very important to understand that if you want to live a long and healthy life and you want to achieve your goals, you have to be an outstanding human being.

You must be a good person. Because if you are not good as a person, you are selling the world short of your own value. No one in this world can provide the value that you provide because only you have the outlook of the world that you have. You see the world differently than everyone else. Everyone has their own vision, their own set of eyes, their own way that they see the world and their place in this universe. And it's up to us as an individual to really define who we are.

In the following art, you can see exactly what I mean:

- The cloud is us.

- The raindrops are our thoughts.

- The seeds are our actions.

- The sprout of the plant is our results.

The cloud and rain combined allow the seeds to grow into the sprout. Likewise, we can use our thoughts to turn our actions into results! In the work of art I have designed for you, you can fill in the spaces I have provided for you. Raindrops represent your thoughts, so you can write one thought of yours in one drop of rain. Seeds represent your actions, so you can write the actions you want to take to turn your thoughts into reality into each of the seeds in the art.

Remember, not all your thoughts may convert into actions. We discard many thoughts as we move forward in life.

Finally, you can fill your desired outcomes within the leaves of the sprout.

Now you know, which thoughts you must turn into action to achieve your desired outcomes!

Chapter 6
Seeds to Trees

Have you ever written down your dreams?

Most of us don't. At every stage of our lives, we set numerous goals and dreams. However, most of the time, these dreams are not well defined and clear. Most of the time we hear people saying,

"I want to become a guitarist."

"I want to become an athlete."

"I want to lose weight."

You know what you want to achieve, but you never try to figure out HOW. If you want to become a guitarist, how will you do that? This HOW gives you a direction. According to a study, people who write down their dreams have ten percent more chance to achieve them than those who don't. When you write down your dreams or goals on a paper, it opens up your thoughts.

It Reminds You of Your Objectives

When you write your dreams down, it serves as a

reminder for you. In the chaos of life, we often forget numerous good ideas which pop up in our mind. The best way to benefit from these ideas is to write them down as soon as they emerge in your mind. Many times just a random thought proves to be a life-changer for you. Develop a habit of writing down your dreams. It will help you in keeping your objective in mind. With constant reminders, you will be more determined to achieve your goals.

It Defines Your Vision

Writing down your goals helps you in defining your vision. When you write down a thought, your brain automatically asks you *Why* and *How*. For example, your goal is to lose weight. You write it down in a journal. When you see it in forms of words, your brain will ask you

Why do you want to lose weight?

And

What are the ways you will adopt?

When you know the answer to this *Why* and *How* you become more confident of achieving it.

It Serves as a Progress Tracker

The written down goals work as a progress checker. For example, you have set a goal, and you also know why and how you will achieve it. The next step is to write down the actions you take to reach your goal. This way, you can keep track of your progress. You are well aware of the actions you have already taken. You know about the strengths and weaknesses of your actions. Failed attempts will keep you from repeating the mistakes. Successful steps will motivate you to try even harder.

"Goals in writing are dreams with deadlines."

-Brian Tracy

I have designed an image for you. The low hanging fruits depict your dreams and goals. The seeds represent your efforts and actions which are mandatory to grow fruits. Each fruit has a blank space. Write down your dreams in the empty space. You will be amazed to see how your mind works to set a defined vision for you.

Chapter 7
The Decision

Have you ever faced a situation in your life, where you just thought about a friend, and they appeared? I am sure that you must have. Many times in our lives, we encounter a situation where things seem to happen magically. We just think about a thing, and it happens. However, it is certainly not magic. This coincidental happening is called synchronicity.

Synchronicity is the occurrence of events in such a way that they appear purely coincidental. These happenings are surprising and unbelievable. When we deeply observe them from a bigger perspective, they prove to be essential pieces that fit ideally into one's life jigsaw puzzle. When you encounter synchronistic events, it is the validation that you are on the correct path. It depicts that you are open to the potential of anything happening in your life.

Synchronicity is a process that connects your heart with soul. Pay close attention to your feelings about certain people, places, and things. Many times you feel a negative vibe from a person you met for the first time. You don't even know them, but you feel something is wrong. It is actually your soul communicating with you. It will never navigate you in the wrong direction. If certain places or people make you feel happy or passionate about life, then divert all your energy toward those things. You might be thinking why I jumped into the discussion about synchronicity when we were busy talking about goals. The reason is, there is a connection between goals and synchronicity. Many times, we want to do more than one thing in our lives. It gets us into a confusing situation where we cannot decide which direction to follow. Synchronicity and the voice of your heart help you in such a condition. It gives you meaningful signals in the form of events that have hidden messages. You have to decode these signals to reach your highest potential. Once you know what your true potential is, it becomes easier to achieve your goals.

How to Increase Synchronicity in Life

Think about the things you want to do in your life. For example, you love singing, painting, and writing. You believe that you have a passion for doing all of these things, but you want to make your career in any one of them. How will you decide what to do? Synchronicity is your answer here. It helps you make the biggest decisions of your life.

Set Intention

Set an intention that you want to embrace any one of your three passions. Now closely observe the events that occur in your life. Analyze the opportunities that are open for you. Try to read between the lines. Notice the direction your life is taking you to. Once you are able to observe these things deeply, you will automatically grasp which is the right path for you.

Here, a question can emerge in your mind about why I am restricting you to achieve one goal only. Well, this is not the case. You may set and achieve several goals if you believe you have the potential. However, you can't do all of these things simultaneously. There is a right time to do everything. Synchronicity helps you identify what the best thing to do at a specific time is.

Let Go of the Limitations

Many times, life gives us an opportunity to reach our highest potential, but we lose it. We believe that things should happen in a certain way, and hence we are not ready to get out of our comfort zone. To benefit from synchronicity, we must eliminate the limiting beliefs from our lives. Instead of becoming overwhelmed with the fear of possible failure, we should focus on what we want to achieve in our lives.

Let Go of the Outcome

Many people might confuse synchronicity with success. Synchronicity is not magic. It is just a thought process which makes you aware of the possibilities and opportunities. It just lets you know that it is the right time to do a particular task. However, you will have to struggle and work hard to reach your goal. You may encounter rejections and failures. So, it is better not to focus on your desired outcome. Just go with the flow and keep working hard. When you are determined to achieve something in your life, the universe opens unlimited ways for you. Remember the Law of Attraction. Never hesitate in trying.

Understanding your true potential is one of the vital steps in goal setting. Never lose hope if you don't succeed in the first go. You can explore opportunities until the day you are alive. Keep up the hard work and struggle. If you want to cultivate synchronicity in your life, try to strengthen your attention and self-control with the help of yoga and meditation. The more attentive and observant you are, the more you can sustain synchronicity, which may open doors for you beyond your imagination.

Always keep your energy going forth into setting actionable goals.

Some say risk nothing, try only for the sure thing,
Others say nothing gambled nothing gained,
Go all out for your dream.
Life can be lived either way, but for me,
I'd rather try and fail than never try at all, you see.
Some say "Don't ever fall in love,
Play the game of life wide open,
Burn your candle at both ends."
But I say, "No! It's better to have loved and lost,
Than never to have loved at all, my friend."
When many moons have gone by,
And you are alone with your dreams of yesteryear,
All your memories will bring you cheer.
You'll be satisfied, succeed or fail, win or lose,
Knowing the right path, you did choose.
-William F. O'Brien

Chapter 8
The Magic of Goal Setting

Can you expect an elementary school child to appear in a college exam?

You must be thinking what a stupid question it is. We all understand it is not possible. However, when we set our goals, we expect overnight results. When we don't see any progress, we lose hope and give up on trying. Big goals cannot be achieved at once. You have to take small steps to summit the peak.

Setting short term goals for smaller periods of time makes you more adaptable. You can easily alter your actions according to the changing circumstances. Focusing too much on a long-term goal can leave you exhausted after some time.

For example, your goal for the next year is to write a book. This is your long-term goal. If you don't set short term steps, you may end up with a lot of scattered information. You can start by setting your monthly targets. Your initial target should be deciding on the genre of the book and creating an overall outline. At this step, you will decide:

- Who will be your audience?
- What message do you want to convey?
- How many chapters do you want to incorporate?
- What should be the length of each chapter?

At this step, forget about everything else. Don't go into the details of the material of each chapter. Focus your energy on the first step only. When you are done with the first step, move ahead with the second step. It can be writing the introduction and first chapter. Now all your attention should be on these two things only. When you work in such a way, you become clearer and more confident. If something doesn't work, you can alter your action plan at the initial stages without wasting much time.

I have been a part of different multi-level marketing companies. A couple of months ago, I developed an idea that if I can work well for these companies, why can't I do for myself. I decided to set up my own business and earn twenty thousand dollars. This was my ultimate goal. I wrote it in a notebook and set my first short term goal of three months. I decided that in the first three months, I will

- Devote my time to approach different prospective clients and

- Set the price for my products according to the value it delivers

I stayed fixated on this goal and worked tirelessly. Within a period of two months, I made a number of good clients and eighteen thousand dollars. Though my first short term goal was not to earn any amount, it eventually helped me in getting closer to my ultimate goal.

Always set your goals according to your skills and capabilities. I would suggest you set simpler goals and work hard to over-deliver. When you deliver more than you promised, you can win the trust of your clients. It can greatly help you to grow your business.

Goals Are Never Realistic

"You need to aim beyond what you are capable of. You must develop a complete disregard for where your abilities end. Try to do things that you're incapable of... If you think you're incapable of running a company, make that your aim... Make your vision of where you want to be a reality. Nothing is impossible."

-Paul Arden

Your ultimate goal should be something out of your comfort zone. As we discussed in the last chapter that opportunists always think out of the box. It is generally said that your goal should be realistic. However, I don't believe in that. All the great inventions are a result of unrealistic goals. About fifty years ago, no one had ever thought about video calls. It seemed to be an impossible concept. However, the person who introduced this technology dared to make this their goal. Nothing can be real until it is done for the first time. I want my readers to believe that you can do anything if you are determined. You just need to put your unrealistic thought on a sheet of paper to make it realistic.

Set Your Goals in a Peaceful Environment

Imagine, you are at the gym right now and running on a treadmill. I ask you to think about an important matter of your life and come up with an action plan. Can you do it? Of course not. You can't run a thought process in a crowded and noisy environment. Your life goals are not something mediocre. They are the essence of your life. When you are on your road to set goals, make sure you sit in a relaxed environment. We have to play different roles in our life, such as a brother or sister, spouse, sibling, friend, and employee. We get overinvolved in fulfilling our responsibilities related to different roles. We don't realize, but we begin forgetting ourselves. I don't ask you not to perform your responsibilities. However, taking out time for your own self is vital to lead a prosperous life.

Find some peaceful place. Any place close to nature is better, such as a beach or forest. Make sure you are away from your children, spouse, and anyone else. You can play some soft music or anything which can soothe your nerves. Music plays an important role in stimulating your mind. It helps you in enhancing your creativity. When you are alone with your thoughts, you become more focused. Your productivity is at its peak when you have complete peace of mind.

Chapter 9
Your Next Steps

"Vision without action is merely a dream. Action without vision just passes the time. Vision with action can change the world."

-Joel A. Barker

In the previous two chapters, we talked a lot about goals and their importance. Imagine, you have documented all of your short- and long-term goals. You are quite clear about what you want to achieve. Now, what's next? If you think, you have played your part, and now you can lie on your bed, you are wrong. The real struggle starts after you have decided on your goals. If you have set goals for yourself, only YOU can turn them into reality. No one else will come to do you a favor. Goals without actions are like an empty glass.

No matter how beautiful the glass is, it can never quench your thirst until you fill it with water, preferably Kangen. In the previous chapter, I suggested you sit in a calm and peaceful environment to think about your dreams. This practice works for actions too. You must write down the actions you will take to pursue your dreams. For example, your ultimate goal is to lose twenty pounds. You will begin by breaking down your goal into small targets. You set a short-term goal to lose two pounds every month. Now you must decide what actions you will take to reach the first step. You may do it by joining a gym and starting a balanced diet. Your action can be anything depending upon your condition and interest. After a month, track your progress. If you think this plan works for you, you can carry on. However, if you couldn't reach your first milestone, there must be some lacking in your action.

Try to figure out what made your action unsuccessful. If you did your best and still couldn't lose the weight, you need to alter your actions. If you couldn't accomplish your goal because of your own laziness, you must change your behavior. It is not necessary to work alone. You can get some help from your family and friends, or you can go for professional counseling as well. Dedication is the key

Thoughts Which Limit Your Actions

"I've learned that fear limits you and your vision. It serves as blinders to what may be just a few steps down the road for you. The journey is valuable, but believing in your talents, your abilities, and your self-worth can empower

you to walk down an even brighter path. Transforming fear
into freedom - how great is that?"

-Soledad O'Brien

Goal setting is all about thinking out of the box. If you set a challenging goal, the actions to achieve it should also be extraordinary. Many times, we are eager to do something, but we don't. Our limiting thoughts and fear of failure keep us from taking action. Let's connect to the weight loss example. Your goal is amazing. However, you are afraid of taking action because of the following recurring thoughts:

What if I don't lose weight even after exercising and dieting?

People will mock me if I don't lose weight.

How will I survive without pizza?

My friends say I can't do it.

These are called limiting thoughts. They restrain you from taking action. Even though your goal is good, you can't achieve it because of your fears. When you work on something bigger, eliminate *What Ifs* from your dictionary. If you search on the internet, you will find a lot of ways to overcome your fears and limiting thoughts. It will suggest you do yoga, meditation, therapy, and what not. All these ways are indeed beneficial, not only for your fears but also for your overall health. However, I have a small exercise for you. It will help you in eliminating all restraining thoughts from your mind.

Sit in a peaceful environment. Take a sheet of paper and write down one of your biggest goals or dreams for the coming year. Now think about the actions you must take to turn your dream into a reality. Write down these actions also on the same sheet. You will notice that as soon as you wrote down the actions, some limiting beliefs emerge in your mind. Take another piece of paper and jot down all those thoughts which frighten you.

Once you have put down these thoughts on a paper, they are no longer inside your mind. You have successfully eliminated them from your brain. Rip up this paper and throw away the pieces. Make sure you must destroy it completely. Even the torn pieces must not return to you. Never look back and begin working on your goal. You may be wondering how such a simple exercise can do the job. But it changes your life. You need to give it a try.

Darren Rowse is a blogger, speaker, and consultant. He says,

"Do the uncomfortable. Become comfortable with these acts. Prove to yourself that your limiting beliefs die a quick death if you will simply do what you feel uncomfortable doing."

Chapter 10
Impossible Is Nothing

Do you know most of us are disserving the world by being in it?

You might be wondering how I can say this.

A vast majority of us live our lives based on the American Dream. We have learned that if we are born in a middle-class family, we are bound to live this life. After graduating from high school, most of the teens plan to go to a college and get a job. They take out large student loans to pay their tuition fee. They have to take out a mortgage to buy a house. Eventually, they end up working for thirty to forty years to pay off all the debts. The most interesting fact is that most of us do the jobs which we don't like at all.

Is this the way to utilize this beautiful gift from God called life?

We are not meant to live this way. God has sent us in this world with a purpose. We are here to bring a change, not only in our lives but also in the lives of other people. We dream for a lavish and luxurious life, but we are not willing to take any risks. Especially, millennials want to achieve everything without struggle and hard work. If we really want to be successful, we must get out of this mentality. I have come across many people in my life who want to do something, but they don't. They bury their dreams because they think they can't do it. They don't even bother trying. I wonder why people lack self-confidence. We get disheartened when someone degrades us. However, we don't realize that we spend our entire life in disrespecting ourselves by doubting our abilities. If you don't regard yourself, how can you expect others to praise you?

Let's assume you fantasize about becoming a boxer, but you wear eyeglasses. Will you give up on this dream?

You must not. Every problem has a solution. You can get LASIK surgery done. You can join a gym to build your body and then strive to pursue your dream. Believe me, if you are determined for something, you will find unlimited ways to do it. You fear to speak of your ideas because you think people will ridicule you. You find it hard to tell someone that you like them because they may reject you. These fears paralyze our true capabilities. I believe that you are only one decision away from a completely different life. I have shared this idea in chapter five also. This thought became the reason for writing this book. One day I was standing on the balcony at a hotel in Panama City Beach. It is a felony in Florida to spit or throw anything off of a balcony. I thought to myself, if I spat or threw anything off of this balcony right now, I would literally become a felon in a matter of a few minutes. It meant I was one loogie away from ending up in prison for a couple of years. If a wrong step can transform my life negatively, why can't a good step, change it in a positive way? I immediately decided to write a book to convey to people that they are in charge of change in their lives. It all comes down to developing the self-confidence in yourself. I want you to be the best that you can be. If you don't strive to be the best you devalue your worth.

We have talked a lot about writing your goals and action plans. I want you to make it your credo,

"If I can write this, it is possible. If it is possible, I can achieve it."

Repetition is the Key

"Repetition of the same thought or physical action develops into a habit which, repeated frequently enough, becomes an automatic reflex."

-Norman Vincent Peale

We are generally impatient when it comes to being successful or achieving our goals. We want everything in a single try. If it was that easy, everyone could do it. You find it difficult. It shows that you are trying to achieve something bigger. There are no shortcuts for success. If you really want it, you need to do it repeatedly and constantly. Take the example of Wright brothers who made it possible for you to fly. Do you think they created an airplane overnight? It took them years of hard work and painful failures to get anywhere close to powered flight. If they had given up in a single try, the world would have never known their names. So believe it that if it is worth achieving, it is worth doing more than once.

Do What You Think You Can't Do

If you have a goal which you think is impossible, write it down. If you think it is out of your realm of possibility, I will ask you to write it tens or hundreds of times. It has emerged in your mind. It depicts that you are meant to do it.

In chapter three, I discussed the renowned speaker Grant

Cardone. I am in love with one of his books, *The 10x Rule.*
The book says

- You should set goals for yourself that are ten times
  greater than what you believe you can accomplish.

- You should create an action plan which is ten times
  bigger than what you believe is imperative to reach
  your milestone.

- We lose interest because we don't set higher
  goals. Setting sky-high goals and taking gigantic
  actions is the only way to fulfill your true potential[8].

You will find five blank pages at the end of this chapter.
I have designed this book to be your handbook, your diary,
your guide, and your way to change your life. Keep this
book with you wherever you go. Whenever an inspiring
thought or idea comes to your mind, immediately write it
down on these blank pages.

You might be asking yourself why you should keep this
book with you when a simple diary or notebook can do the
job. When you take this book out of your handbag or
folder, the title will motivate you. You will recall

---

[8]James Clear. (2019). The 10X Rule by Grant Cardone. Website. Retrieved
from: https://jamesclear.com/book-summaries/10x-rule

92

everything you read in it. You will feel more enthusiastic about striving to get to the peak.

CAMERON WHEELER

ONE DECISION AWAY

_____
_____
_____
_____
_____
_____
_____
_____
_____
_____
_____
_____
_____
_____
_____
_____
_____
_____
_____
_____
_____
_____
_____
_____

_____
_____
_____
_____
_____
_____
_____
_____
_____
_____
_____
_____
_____
_____
_____
_____
_____
_____
_____
_____
_____
_____
_____
_____

CAMERON WHEELER

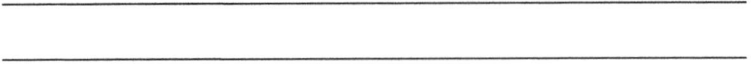

Chapter 11
Peace & Prosperity

"This life is for loving, sharing, learning, smiling, caring, forgiving, laughing, hugging, helping, dancing, wondering, healing, and even more loving. I choose to live life this way. I want to live my life in such a way that when I get out of bed in the morning, the devil says, 'aw shit, he's up!"

-Steve Maraboli

Sometimes I feel like my life is a roller-coaster. It is full of ups and downs. However, I am happy that I learned how to stay firm at downs and relish the ups. This is the last chapter of this book, but this is not the ending. I don't want you to put this book back on the shelf after reading it. I want the end of this book to be the beginning of your new life. You can start fresh in this new life by writing new goals to follow on each page of this book.

Carry it with you at all times and make sure you never stop reminding yourself of your life's objectives and how you plan on achieving them. You are going to lead a purposeful life from now on. To me, this is not merely a book; this is a cause for helping others. I have shared everything that I have experienced in my life thus far. I had to struggle a lot to get out of a disastrous life. I was fortunate enough to find some people who not only mentored me but also played a big role in transforming my life. God sent them in my life as a blessing. Now I want to be a blessing for others. I want this to be a never-ending chain. You read this book, and if you learned something, play your role to bring a change in someone else's life. My mantra is

"Share your experience and add value to people's lives."

I want it to be your mantra too. I want my readers to connect with me on Facebook and Instagram. We will create a group with an aim to help others. This cause should never end. I have been through several adverse phases in my life. I know how it feels when you have to fight the battle of life alone. I want to assure you that the good days are not too far away.

"I know it seems hard sometimes but remember one thing. Through every dark night, there's a bright day after that. So, no matter how hard it gets, stick your chest out, keep your head up... and handle it."

-Tupac Shakur

If you ever feel dejected and heartbroken, you can reach

me anytime. I am more than happy to be your friend, mentor, confidant, and the one you can trust. Feel free to email me and share an extract from each chapter which you liked the most. Join hands with me in my cause to bring a pleasant change in people's life.

"Remember that the happiest people are not those getting more, but those giving more."

-H. Jackson Brown Jr

ONE DECISION AWAY

www.ingramcontent.com/pod-product-compliance
Lightning Source LLC
Chambersburg PA
CBHW072203090426
42740CB00012B/2366